TEACHING BIBLE TRUTHS WITH ARTS & CRAFTS

Celebrate!

THE HOLIDAYS WITH SCRIPTURE

by Dorla Schlitt

Nashville, Tennessee ©1998 by Dorla Schlitt

All rights reserved

Printed in the United State of America

0-8054-0245-4

Unless otherwise stated, Scripture is from the King James Version.

Other Scripture marked NIV, is from The Holy Bible, New International Version,

©1973, 1978, 1984 by International Bible Society.

Table of Contents

THEME	ACTIVITY	PAGE

Celebrate God's Love

VALENTINE BIRD

Valentine's Day is a holiday that celebrates love and caring. Traditionally the valentine "heart" is used as a symbol of love, caring, and friendship. Remind the children that though it is important to tell our friends and loved ones we care about them "our actions speak louder than our words." Undoubtedly the greatest example of this was when Jesus gave his own life for us.

Spend some time talking with the children about instances when you have observed them caring for others. Perhaps it was a sister or brother. Help them think of some ways they could show their love for their friends, relatives, and neighbors. Help them understand that in serving others they are displaying Jesus' love.

Greater love hath no man than this,
that a man lay down his life for his friends.
John 15:13

A friend loveth at all times.
Proverbs 17:17

These things I command you,
that ye love one another.
John 15:17

Valentine's Day

VALENTINE BIRD (CONTINUED)

- construction paper: red, pink, white
- patterns
- glue
- scissors
- pencil
- yarn
- paper punch

procedure

1. Use the patterns to cut out different sized hearts from colored construction paper.
2. To form the bird: 1 large heart for the body, 1 small heart for the tail, 1 large heart cut in two for wings, 1 large heart cut in two for the head, 1 tiny heart for the eye.
3. Punch a hole at the top and hang the valentine bird with yarn.

activities

1. Assemble several valentine birds together and make a mobile. Use 2 twigs bound together at their centers to form a cross. Hang a valentine bird from each end and the center with a needle and thread.
2. Glue a valentine bird on the outside of a white paper sack. Fill the sack with popcorn, cookies, and candy. Deliver the sack to a shut in or a special loved one.
3. Make a small valentine bird. Copy the Scripture onto the body of the bird and use it as a bookmark.

Assembled Valentine Bird

VALENTINE BIRD PATTERNS

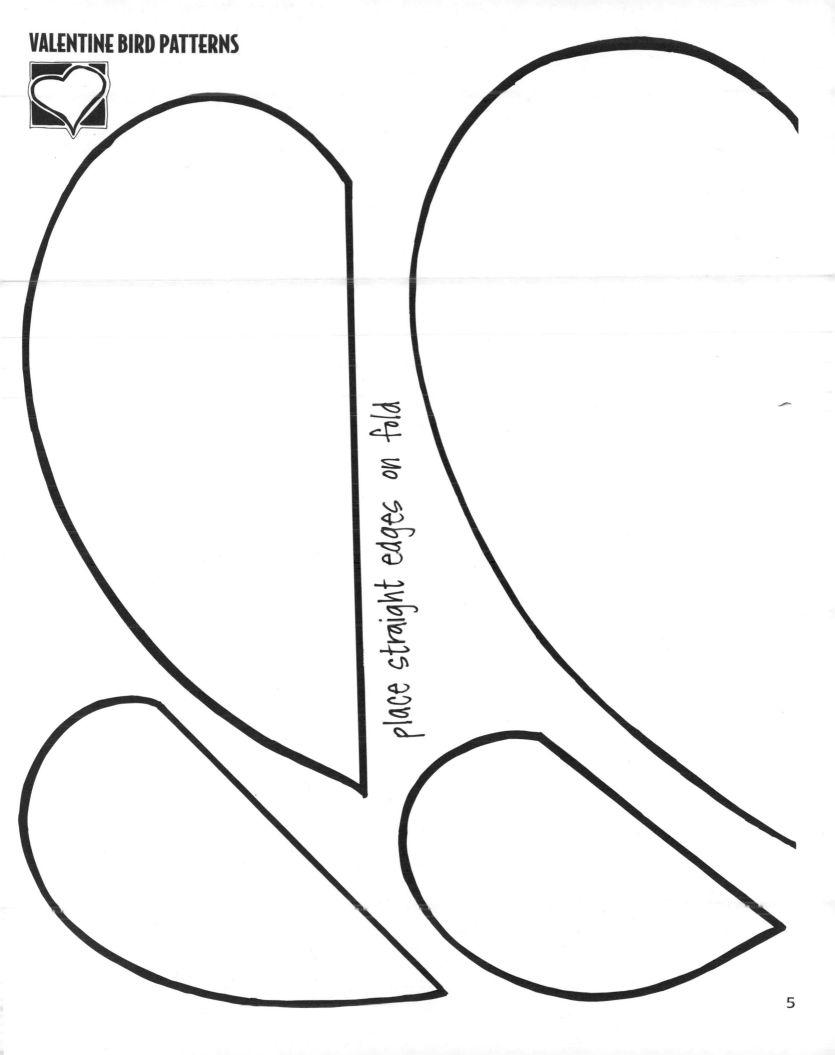

place straight edges on fold

Walking in God's Love

HEARTS OF LOVE BANNER

Candy hearts are everywhere! Children love to read the little saying on each and pop it in their mouth. This simple valentine craft provides paper hearts with something to read on each—a Scripture! It also provides the opportunity to talk with your children about love—the love God has for us and the love He wants us to have for each other.

Explain to your children that love is not always a feeling but a choice, an attitude. Romans 5:8 tells us that God chose to love us even while we were sinners. We, too, have opportunities to choose to love others even when they disappoint us or hurt us. God's love can flow through us to other people if we will let it.

God's love for us is deep, constant, and always seeks our good. This same love is poured into our hearts. God wants it to flow out towards others as the fruit of His Spirit. We are to love others unselfishly and in obedience to God's word. Share with the children your struggles in learning to forgive and love others in spite of hurts and disappointments. Ask them to share their struggles and encourage them to forgive and love.

Scripture

Love is patient, love is kind. It does not envy, it does not boast, it is not proud. It is not rude, it is not self-seeking, it is not easily angered, it keeps no record of wrongs. Love does not delight in evil but rejoices with the truth. It always protects, always trusts, always hopes, always perseveres. Love never fails. But where there are prophecies, they will cease; where there are tongues, they will be stilled; where there is knowledge, it will pass away. 1 Corinthians 13:4-8, NIV

Herein is love, not that we loved God, but that he loved us, and sent his Son to be the propitiation for our sins. Beloved, if God so loved us, we ought also to love one another. No man hath seen God at any time. If we love one another, God dwelleth in us, and his love is perfected in us. 1 John 4:10-12

Valentine's Day

materials

- construction paper: red, pink, white
- scissors
- glue
- pencil
- ruler
- fine tip markers
- paper clip
- tape
- ribbon
- trims
- decorations
- 1"-2" wide ribbon
- small safety pin

procedure

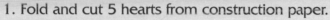

1. Fold and cut 5 hearts from construction paper.
2. Cut two strips of construction paper 2" wide. Glue the ends together to form one long strip.
3. Choose a Scripture about "love" for each heart.
4. Use a ruler and pencil to draw guidelines on the front of each heart. Copy a Scripture neatly onto each heart using a pencil.
5. Go over the pencil with fine tip markers.
6. Decorate each heart.
7. Glue the hearts to the long strip of construction paper leaving room at the top for the bow.
8. Make a bow with the ribbon. Anchor the ribbon to the top of the paper strip with glue or a small safety pin.
9. On the back of the paper strip tape the paper clip in place so the banner can be hung.

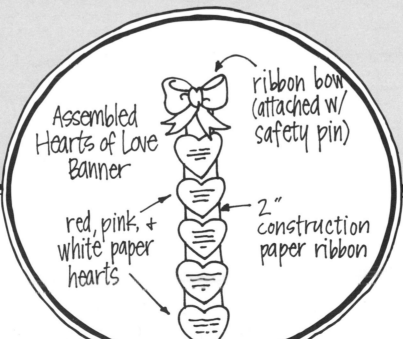

Assembled Hearts of Love Banner

ribbon bow (attached w/ safety pin)

red, pink, + white paper hearts

2" construction paper ribbon

SPLIT PAPER VALENTINE

Valentine's Day is fast approaching and the children are excited to learn how to make pretty paper hearts. Use this easy craft to teach them how to make a paper heart and also use it as an opportunity to get your children thinking about the heart—the spiritual heart of man as well as the physical heart.

The heart is the chief organ of the physical body and occupies the most important place in the human system. The flow of blood must go through the heart to be cleaned and then out again to every living cell with life sustaining oxygen. The condition of the heart has a major influence on the health of the body and the condition of life.

So it is with the spiritual heart of man. It is the center of our inward life. It is who we really are inside. Only by the cleansing blood of Jesus Christ and the Word of God can man's inward heart be changed. A heart that is changed by Jesus Christ and the Word of God will eventually effect every area of a believer's life. The health of a man's spirit, soul, and body is dependent on the condition of his spiritual heart. It effects his entire life.

purpose

Above all else, guard your heart, for it is the wellspring of life.
Proverbs 4:23, NIV

scripture

For man looketh on the outward appearance,
but the LORD looketh on the heart.
1 Samuel 16:7

For the word of God is living and active. Sharper than any
double-edged sword, it penetrates even to dividing soul and spirit,
joints and marrow; it judges the thoughts and attitudes of the heart.
Hebrews 4:12, NIV

Valentine's Day

materials

- construction paper: red, pink, white
- scissors
- glue
- pencil
- markers

procedure

1. Choose two colors of construction paper.
2. Fold one piece of construction paper in half for a card.
3. Fold the second piece of construction paper and draw half of a heart along the edge of the paper. The center of the heart is along the fold line.
4. Cut along the pencil line—not along the fold line.
5. Unfold the heart. Draw pencil lines to divide the heart into sections. Cut along the pencil lines.
6. Lay the pieces of the heart on the front of the card leaving small spaces between the pieces. Glue in place.
7. Write a meaningful message in pencil inside the card. Use a ruler for straight lines.
8. Go over the pencil in fine tip marker.

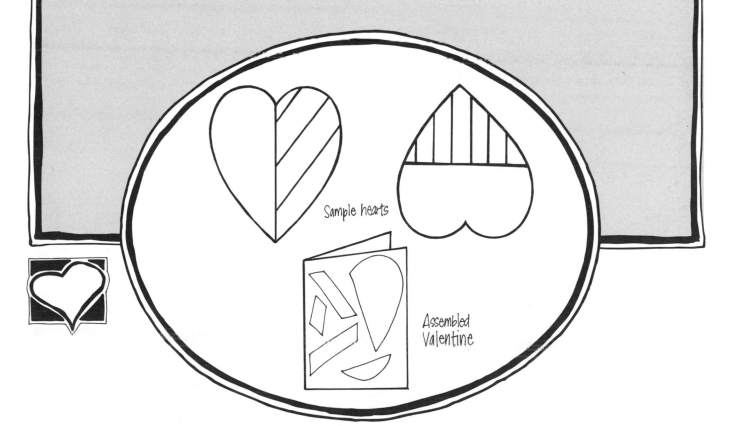

Sample hearts

Assembled Valentine

We are the Body of Christ

HEART BEAT MOBILE

This simple craft provides an opportunity for two children to work together to help one another complete the task.

Talk with the children about what it means to be part of the body of Christ. Explain that the physical body is made up of many different parts working together to accomplish a task. Give the example of walking. Walking takes a message sent from the brain by the nerves to the necessary muscles, tendons, and joints in the leg and foot. All must work appropriately together to accomplish the task of walking.

purpose

This is how the Lord wants the members of His spiritual body, the church, to work together. To cooperate means to act or work with others for a common purpose. Our common purpose as the body of Christ is to glorify God. The Bible gives us specific directions in how to do this. The children will use some of these directions to complete this craft.

Scripture

Just as each of us has one body with many members,
and these members do not all have the same function,
so in Christ we who are many form one body,
and each member belongs to all the others.
Romans 12:4-5, NIV

Keep thy heart with all diligence; for out of it are the issues of life.
Proverbs 4:23

Create in me a clean heart, O God; and renew a right spirit within me.
Psalm 51:10

A merry heart doeth good like a medicine. Proverbs 17:22

materials

- construction paper: red, white, pink
- paper punch
- scissors
- pencil
- yarn
- 2 twigs approximately the same length

procedure

1. Fold a piece of construction paper and cut out a heart. Repeat until you have four hearts.
2. Choose 8 different Scriptures to print neatly in pencil on the front and back of each heart.
3. Go over the pencil with a fine tip marker.
4. Punch a hole at the top center of each heart. Secure an equal length of yarn through each hole of each heart.
5. Cross one twig over the center of the other. Secure with yarn.
6. Tie each length of yarn with a heart hanging from it to the ends of the twigs and between the center and end of each twig. All eight hearts will be hanging. You may need to adjust lengths so the mobile will balance properly.

Scripture choices

Ephesians. 4:32
Galatians 6:2
James 5:16
Philippians. 2:3
Romans 13:10
Galatians 5:14

Colossians 3:13
Romans 12:10
Romans 14:13

Galatians 6:10
Ephesians 4:25
Matthew 7:12
I John 3:18
I Thessalonians 5:11
Ephesians 4:29

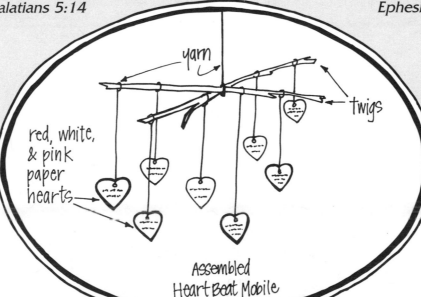

Assembled
Heart Beat Mobile

Celebrate Jesus' Resurrection

RESURRECTION POSTER

The promise of salvation and eternal life through the death, burial, and resurrection of Jesus Christ is awesome!

Read and discuss with your children John chapters 18-20. Explain to them the great work Jesus did by being obedient to the Father. Point out that the Bible speaks of other men who had been raised from the dead but no man other than Jesus was resurrected into eternal life. Point out to them that the Bible tells us that the same Spirit which raised Jesus from the dead dwells within each Believer and will also resurrect us to eternal life. Eternal life is ours through Jesus Christ! What a reason to celebrate!

This fun poster activity will provide the opportunity for the children to choose their own simple Scripture and spend time thinking about what it means and how best to illustrate its message.

purpose

Scripture

*But if the Spirit of him that raised up Jesus from the dead dwell in you,
he that raised up Christ from the dead shall also quicken your
mortal bodies by his Spirit that dwelleth in you.*
Romans 8:11

*Jesus said unto her, I am the resurrection, and the life:
he that believeth in me, though he were dead, yet shall he live.*
John 11:25

Easter

materials

- large sheet of posterboard
- large sheet of newsprint or newspaper
- stencils (made from patterns)
- ruler
- markers
- construction paper
- paper punch
- coloring books
- tracing paper
- patterns
- trims
- 1 yd. 1" ribbon for each child

preparation

1. Construct a sample poster to stimulate ideas.

   Example: a 3-D poster, a collage poster

2. Prepare patterns and stencils.

1. Choose a simple phrase for the focus of the poster.
2. Choose from the patterns, coloring book pictures or any other creative ideas to help decorate the poster.
3. Use the newsprint or newspaper to plan the placement of letters and illustrations. Remember proper spacing and balance. Check the rough draft with an adult.
4. Use the rough draft for reference and begin work on the posterboard.
5. Lightly sketch in pencil the letters. Trace over the pencil with markers. Be sure the lettering is bold.
6. Use trims or construction paper trim for the bottom edge.
7. Punch a hole large enough on each side of the top edge for the ribbon to slip through. Tie the ends together in a bow. Hang.

procedure

phrase choices

It Is Finished!
The Lord Reigneth!
He Is Risen!
Rejoice Evermore!
Let Us Be Glad!
He Is Alive!

Allelulia!
King of Kings and Lord of Lords!
Thou Art Worthy, O Lord!
Great is the Lord!
I Am The Resurrection And The Life!

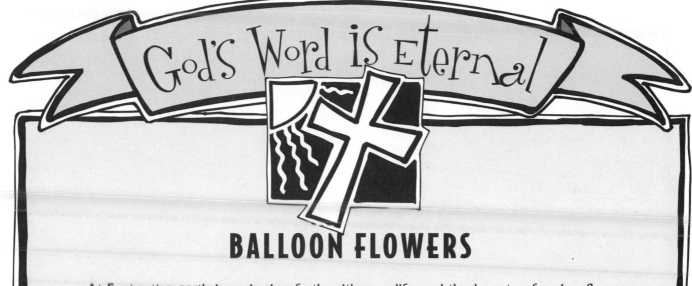

God's Word is Eternal

BALLOON FLOWERS

At Easter the earth is springing forth with new life and the beauty of spring flowers. Use this craft to create a pretty spring flower which reinforces the Scripture Isaiah 40:8.

In reading the verse together explain that the word "eternal" means God's word is forever the same. It will not change. It is the same for all people, all times, and all places. Point out to your children that though flowers fade and fall away God's word is true forever. It is eternal.

Talk with your children about the similarity between what happens to a seed planted in the earth and our physical body which is buried in the earth at death. Explain that the seed's outside shell dies and falls away allowing the life within the seed to spring forth as a flower. Help them understand that because we have eternal life through Jesus Christ our physical bodies will die and fall away allowing our spirit and soul to be released to live forever. Unlike the flower that eventually fades our soul and spirit will receive a new and glorious body at the resurrection of the dead. This body will never die.

purpose

Scripture

The grass withereth, the flower fadeth:
but the word of our God shall stand for ever.
Isaiah 40:8

The body that is sown is perishable, it is raised imperishable;
it is sown in dishonor, it is raised in glory; it is sown in weakness,
it is raised in power; it is sown a natural body, it is raised a spiritual body.
If there is a natural body, there is also a spiritual body.
I Corinthians 15:42-44, NIV

Easter

materials

- 12" round balloon—any color
- 9" x 12" construction paper—any color
- patterns
- paint stir stick
- fine tip markers
- scissors
- glue
- masking tape
- green construction paper

procedure

1. Draw around the petal pattern onto any color of construction paper. Cut out.
2. Cut the slits in the center of the paper petals.
3. Add color to the paper petal with markers.
4. Blow up the balloon and tie the end.
5. Insert the tied end of the balloon through the slits of the paper petals. Secure it with a piece of masking tape.
6. Draw around the stem and leaf patterns on the green construction paper. Cut out and glue each to the paint stick.
7. Anchor the flower to the stem with masking tape on the back.
8. Neatly print the Scripture down the stem of the flower: "The word of our God stands forever." Isaiah 40:8, NIV.

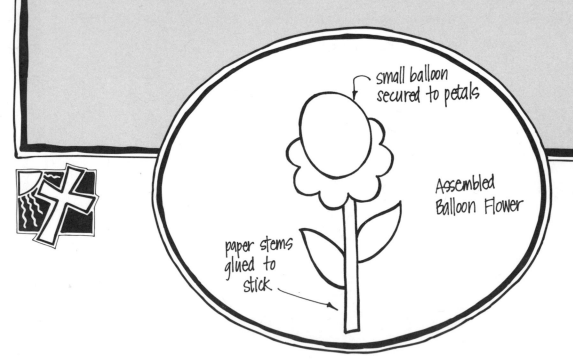

small balloon secured to petals

Assembled Balloon Flower

paper stems glued to stick

BALLOON FLOWER PATTERN

leaves:
cut 4

stem:
cut 2

place on fold

petals:
cut 1

God Forgives

STAINED GLASS CROSS

This simple craft is a reminder to the children of the great work Jesus accomplished through the cross. What was the great work? The redemption of all mankind was accomplished at the cross by Jesus Christ.

Explain to the children that the word "redemption" means "to get back by paying a fee." Through the cross and crucifixion Jesus paid the ultimate price. His blood shed for us provided the final sacrifice for the forgiveness of sin and made it possible for mankind to be reconciled to God. The cross is symbolic of Jesus' crucifixion. Jesus' crucifixion is central to Christianity.

Read and discuss the parable of the rich young ruler found in Mark 10:17-22. The cross of Jesus brought redemption to the world. The cross we are to carry is to willingly give up our right to ourselves to Jesus Christ. What was Jesus trying to explain to the rich young ruler?

purpose

scripture

*For he has rescued us from the dominion of darkness and
brought us into the kingdom of the Son he loves,
in whom we have redemption, the forgiveness of sins.
Colossians 1:13-14, NIV*

*And being found in fashion as a man, he humbled himself,
and became obedient unto death, even the death of the cross.
Philippians 2:8*

*For God was pleased to have all his fullness dwell in him, and through him to reconcile to himself all things, whether things on earth or things in heaven, by making peace through his blood, shed on the cross.
Colossians 1:19-20, NIV*

Easter

materials

- cross pattern
- 8 1/2" x 11" colored construction paper
- 8" x 10" piece of wax paper
- multi-colored tissue paper
- watercolor brush
- small water container
- newspaper
- glue
- plastic bags
- water
- scissors
- pencil

preparation

1. Cut each color of tissue paper into 1" squares and store them in plastic bags.
2. Make enough cross patterns for your group.
3. Prepare the glue mixture by adding water to the glue in a small container. When it is a watery consistency and spreads easily it is ready.
4. Cover the work area with newspapers.

procedure

1. Trace around the cross in the center of 1 sheet of colored construction paper. Carefully cut out only the cross.
2. Lay the sheet of paper with the cut out cross on top of another sheet of colored construction paper. Trace around the edge of the cross opening onto the 2nd sheet. Cut out only the cross on the 2nd sheet. With both sheets together the cross cut outs should match up exactly.
3. Lay one of the colored construction paper sheets with the cut out cross over the wax paper. Trace around the edge of the cross opening onto the wax paper.
4. Lay the construction paper sheets aside.
5. Lay a tissue square anywhere on the wax paper cross drawing.
6. Use the water color brush to dab into the glue mixture and brush the glue mixture completely over the tissue square. Completely saturate it—no part left dry.
7. Take a second tissue square that is a different color than the first and repeat the procedure being sure to overlap edges of the first tissue square.
8. Continue the procedure until the entire cross is covered with saturated tissue squares. Be sure the tissue paper edges are all overlapped and extend over the edges of the penciled cross. Let dry.
9. Lay the construction paper cross cut out over the wax paper covered in tissue squares. Be sure the tissue paper covers all of the cross cut out space. Glue the wax paper to the construction paper.
10. Place the second piece of construction paper with the cross cut out on the other side of the wax paper. Be sure the cross cut out matches up. Glue. The wax paper with tissue squares should now be sandwiched between the two construction paper sheets with the cross cut out. The tissue paper squares should be the only things showing in the cross cut out.
11. Use small pieces of scotch tape and secure it to a window. Observe the stained glass effect through the cut out cross.

STAINED GLASS CROSS PATTERN

MOTHER'S DAY COUPON BOOK

Children are never too young to learn the importance of being a servant and appreciating those who serve. Begin by explaining that a servant is one who helps or aides another. Jesus tells us in Mark 10:43-44 that the sign of someone great in the kingdom of God is a person who serves or helps others by meeting their needs and caring for them.

Man's idea of greatness is TO BE SERVED AND RECEIVE FROM OTHERS.

God's idea of greatness is TO SERVE AND TO GIVE TO OTHERS.

Help your children identify those people in their life who serve them. The list might include their Sunday School teacher, their Brownie or Cub Scout leader, their coach, and of course, their parents. Remind them that many times they receive little or no thanks for their efforts. Help your child understand the importance of these people's attitudes of giving regardless of material rewards. As Christians how are we to serve others? We are to serve others as if we were serving Jesus—out of love for Him—no other motive.

Mother's Day is a perfect opportunity for your children to serve or help their mother. A coupon book is one way to do that. Explain that a coupon is a piece of paper that is worth something in money or service. Help your children identify and list services they can do to help Mom (pick up toys, set the table, wash dishes, dust, sweep the floor or sidewalk, clear the table, water the flowers, fold towels, clean sinks or windows, feed a pet, entertain brother or sister). Encourage them in their desire to be good helpers who serve cheerfully.

With good will doing service, as to the Lord, and not to men. Ephesians 6:7

Serve the LORD with gladness: come before his presence with singing. Psalm 100:2

But by love serve one another. Galatians 5:13

purpose

Scripture

materials

- colored construction paper
- patterns
- white paper
- paper punch
- glue markers
- ribbon
- yarn
- trims
- glitter
- sequins
- construction paper scraps

preparation

1. Prepare the patterns.
2. Using the pattern for the coupon sheets cut an appropriate number needed for each child's book.
3. Punch holes in the appropriate place on the coupon sheets.

procedure

1. Choose several services to perform for mother.
2. Copy neatly in pencil one service per page. Illustrate each page. Set aside.
3. Draw around the patterns for the front and back cover on construction paper. Cut them out.
4. Label "Mother's Coupon Book" in pencil on the front cover. Trace over all pencil with fine tip marker.
5. Decorate the front cover.
6. Punch holes at the appropriate places on the front and back cover.
7. Combine all the coupon pages with the front and back cover. Tie through the holes a length of yarn. Tie a bow.

sample coupon

This coupon is payable to _____

for _____

Signed with love

_____

front & back cover

FATHER'S DAY BOOKMARK

What does the word "honor" mean? To honor someone is to show great respect for them.

Discuss with the children ways they can honor their fathers. Help them think of examples of acting courteously, showing consideration, caring for their father's feelings and obeying him. Help them understand that one great way to honor him is to respect his quiet time with Jesus. By allowing him to read his Bible uninterrupted they are honoring him.

Let this simple bookmark, made as a gift, be a reminder to your child of their desire to honor their father.

Also take this time to talk with the children about being a good steward. By using the scraps from the arts and crafts materials, they are using these materials in a productive, useful way.

purpose

Honour thy father and mother; which is the first commandment with promise;
That it may be well with thee, and thou mayest live long on the earth.
Ephesians 6:2-3

Hear the instruction of thy father.
Proverbs 1:8

But glory, honour, and peace,
to every man that worketh good.
Romans 2:10

Scripture

Father's Day

materials

- 4" wax paper square
- paper punch
- glue
- round toothpicks
- fine tip markers
- muffin tin
- construction paper
- newspaper
- construction paper scraps
- old greeting card patterns
- clear contact paper
- 12" narrow ribbon or yarn

preparation

1. Prior to the project punch holes out of construction paper scraps. Sort the colored dots into the muffin tin.
2. Prepare the patterns.
3. Prepare the working area. Cover the table with newspaper. Place the muffin tin and toothpicks on the table along with the wax paper square for glue.

procedure

1. Draw around the two different sized patterns and cut out.
2. Glue the smaller to the larger bookmark.
3. Sketch a design, a small picture, or print Dad's name in pencil.
4. Use a toothpick to dip into the glue. Apply a small dot of glue onto the design. Place a colored dot on top of the glue. Very little glue is needed.
5. Use markers, torn construction paper scraps, or greeting card characters as needed.
6. Cover the bookmark's front and back with clear contact paper.
7. Punch a hole in the center top of the bookmark and tie a colorful ribbon.

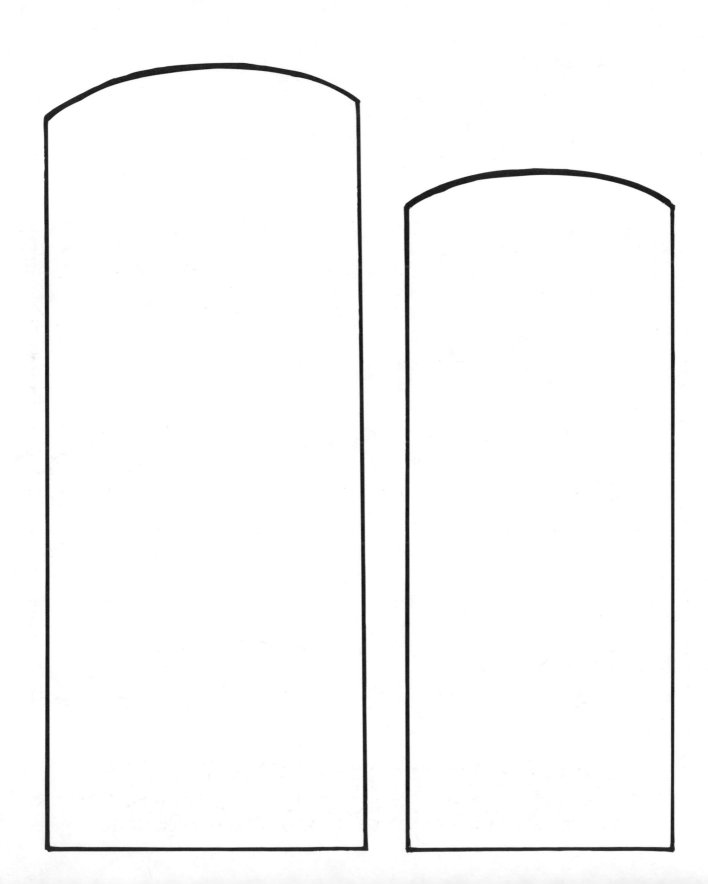

A BLESSING WREATH

Instead of Halloween decorations on your door during the month of October why not focus on God's goodness by making a "Blessing Wreath"?

Begin the activity with a discussion. Talk with your children about the goodness of God and His blessing to your family. Explain that a blessing is a gift, not something earned by doing good or being good. Point out that the greatest blessing we can ever receive from God is to know our need for Jesus and accept Him into our heart as Savior and Lord.

Spend time helping your children identify other blessings from God. Make a list. Remind them that God has blessed or given gifts in all areas of our lives, including things they cannot see with their eyes. These would include faith to believe, love to share, joy in their hearts, and peace in their relationship with God through Jesus Christ.

Finish with an activity time of collecting pictures from magazines, greeting cards, photos, and small cut out drawings they might make themselves of the blessings they listed. Construct a "Blessing Wreath" for each child to take home. Display them on your front door as a witness of God's goodness to your family.

purpose

Scripture

*The LORD, The LORD God, merciful and gracious,
longsuffering, and abundant in goodness and truth.*
Exodus 34:6

*Blessed be the God and Father of our Lord Jesus Christ,
who hath blessed us with all spiritual blessings in heavenly places in Christ.*
Ephesians 1:3

Halloween Alternative

materials

- large paper plate
- large paper clip
- glue
- masking tape
- scissors
- fine tip marker
- pictures from greeting cards
- magazines photos
- small drawings
- construction paper
- fall colors

procedure

1. Trace your hand on several fall colors of construction paper and cut them out.
2. Glue the hands to the outer edge of the paper plate with the palms to the inside edge.
3. Tape the large paper clip to the back of the plate out of sight.
4. In the center of the plate neatly print in pencil: "Truly God is good" (Psalm 73:1). Go over the pencil with a fine tip marker.
5. Cut out several pictures from magazines that exemplify blessings from God and glue them around the center caption. Be careful not to cover the Scripture. Remember you can also use photos, small drawing, or even key words such as "faith" "joy" "love".

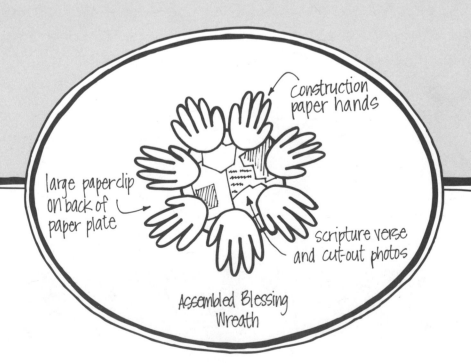

construction paper hands

large paperclip on back of paper plate

scripture verse and cut-out photos

Assembled Blessing Wreath

PINE CONE TURKEY

Use this simple craft near Thanksgiving to encourage children's thankfulness for God's provision. As you explain about a very special pine cone, the children should develop a deeper appreciation of God's goodness, wisdom, and power.

Begin by telling the children that a pine cone is the fruit of the pine tree. Within the pine cone are the seeds that grow into pine trees. One very interesting kind of pine is called the jack pine. This pine tree bears small curved cones that remain closed and hold their seeds for many years. This pine tree is often one of the first trees to grow after a forest fire. The heat from the forest fire causes the cones to open and release tremendous amounts of accumulated seeds. Burned areas of the forests are completely reseeded and can sprout new trees.

God's thinking and planning beforehand provides a way for a forest to be restored to life. Help your children see the similarity between the burned out forest and we who are dead in our sins. Both are hopeless without God's divine intervention. God provides the way for the forest to be restored to life through the pine cone. God provides the way for man to be restored and given eternal life through the person of Jesus Christ.

purpose

You care for the land and water it; you enrich it abundantly.
Psalm 65:9, NIV

Cast all your anxiety on him because he cares for you.
1 Peter 5:7, NIV

Scripture

materials

• pine cone (see pattern page for suggested size)
• lump of Play-Doh™ or modeling clay
• patterns for turkey head, feathers, place card
• construction paper for head and feathers
• white index card
• glue
• scissors

procedure

1. Give each child a pine cone.
2. Draw around the head pattern on construction paper and cut it out.
3. Glue the head into place (see illustration).
4. Draw around the feather pattern on several different colors of construction paper. Cut out the feathers.
5. Glue the feathers into place (see illustration).
6. Use a small amount of clay or Play-Doh™ to form a ball. Press it down slightly and mount the turkey on it.
7. To make the place card fold the white index card in half. Print the name neatly. Place the card next to the turkey.

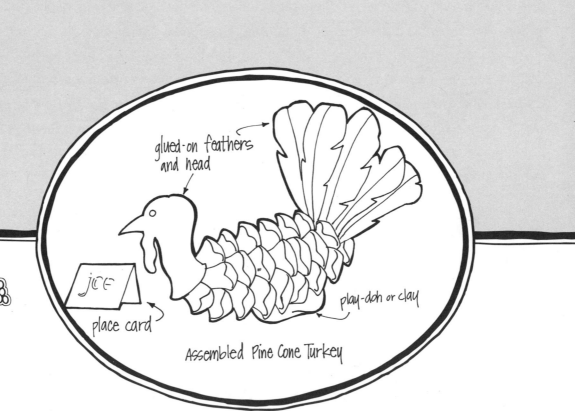

glued-on feathers and head

place card

play-doh or clay

Assembled Pine Cone Turkey

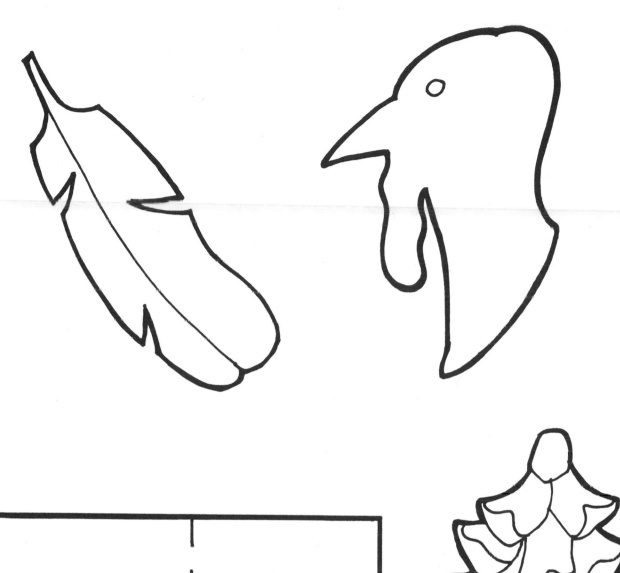

place card

approximate size
of pine cone

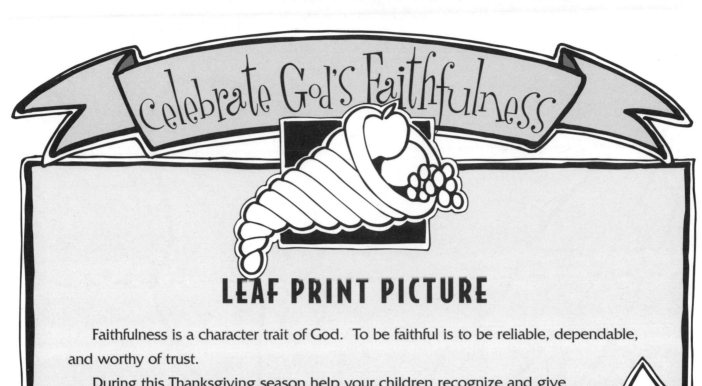

Celebrate God's Faithfulness

LEAF PRINT PICTURE

Faithfulness is a character trait of God. To be faithful is to be reliable, dependable, and worthy of trust.

During this Thanksgiving season help your children recognize and give thanks to God for His faithfulness. Begin by sharing with your children examples of God's faithfulness to you. If possible, take a nature walk and talk about God's faithfulness to His creation. Discuss the change of seasons and the setting and rising of the sun each day. Encourage them to think of other examples of God's faithfulness.

God is faithful, by whom ye were called unto the fellowship of his Son Jesus Christ our Lord.
1 Corinthians 1:9

But my God shall supply all your need according to his riches in glory by Christ Jesus.
Philippians 4:19

If we confess our sins, he is faithful and just to forgive us our sins, and to cleanse us from all unrighteousness.
1 John 1:9

Thanksgiving

materials

- newspapers
- Styrofoam™ egg cartons
- brushes
- water containers
- paper towels
- tempera paints in fall colors
- leaves that are not too dry
- 18" x 12" construction paper
- ruler
- pencil
- fine tip marker

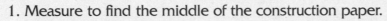

preparation

1. Cover the work area with newspapers.
2. Prepare the painting area with brushes, water containers, and paper towels.
3. Use egg cartons to hold different colors of paint. Set them in place on the covered table.
4. Prepare an area for drying the prints.
5. Print "God is faithful"(1 Corinthians 1:9) on paper for the children to copy.

procedure

1. Measure to find the middle of the construction paper.
2. Use a ruler to lightly draw a straight horizontal line through the center of the construction paper.
3. Neatly print in pencil "God is faithful"(1 Corinthians 1:9) on the line. Trace over the pencil with a fine tip marker.
4. Using a brush to cover the back of one leaf with tempera paint. Carefully lay the leaf paint side down onto the edge of the construction paper. Be sure the entire leaf is on the paper. Press gently and evenly. Remove the leaf.
6. Print another leaf with the same or different color paint next to or overlapping the first leaf. Continue the procedure around the edge of the paper forming a border for the Scripture.
7. Let dry in a safe place. Mount and display.

GOD IS FAITHFUL...
1 COR. 1:9

leaf prints

printed verse.

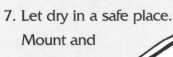

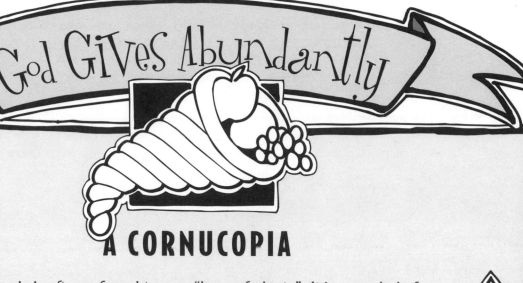

A CORNUCOPIA

A cornucopia is often referred to as a "horn of plenty". It is a symbol of overflowing fullness; abundance. Using the cornucopia in this activity provides an opportunity to talk with your children about all the different kinds of foods God provides for our nutrition and enjoyment.

Spend some time looking through grocery ads in the newspaper or magazines with food pictures in them. Help the children identify the food. Explain the different food groups to them and emphasize the importance of eating a variety of foods to build strong muscles and bodies.

If possible, take a field trip to the grocery. Identifying and classify foods the children like into the main food groups. Discuss with them the abundance we enjoy because of God's blessing on our country.

Talk with the children about why your family should pray before each meal. Help them begin to verbalize their thanksgiving for all the wonderful varieties of good food God gives us in abundance.

For every creature of God is good, and nothing to be refused,
if it be received with thanksgiving:
For it is sanctified by the word of God and prayer
1 Timothy 4:4-5

Unto thee, O God, do we give thanks, unto thee do we give thanks:
for that thy name is near thy wondrous works declare.
Psalm 75:1

O give thanks unto the LORD; call upon his name:
make known his deeds among the people.
Psalm 105:1

Scripture

materials

- cornucopia pattern
- brown construction paper
- construction paper for background
- supermarket food advertisements
- magazines
- scissors
- glue
- fine tip marker
- ruler
- pencil

preparation

1. Make several cornucopia patterns.
2. Collect food advertisements and pictures of food from magazines.

procedure

1. Trace around the cornucopia on the brown construction paper. Cut it out.
2. Cut out colorful fruits, vegetables, meats, dairy products, and grain foods from magazines and food advertisements.
3. Glue the cornucopia to the colored construction paper sheet.
4. Arrange the food pictures in and spilling out of the cornucopia. Glue them to the construction paper.
5. Draw a level ruled line across the top of the paper. Copy neatly one of the two Scriptures in pencil: "We give thanks to You, O God" (Psalm 75:1, NIV) or "Give thanks to the LORD" (Psalm 105:1).
6. Trace over the pencil with a fine tip marker.
7. Mount and display.

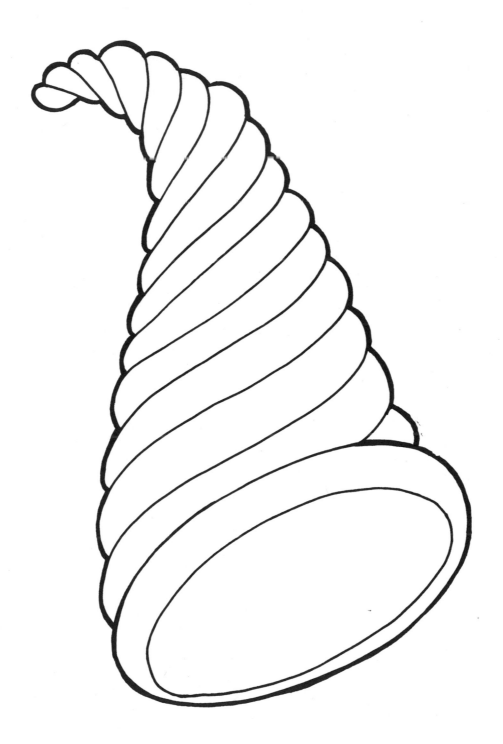

CELEBRATION BANNER

Christmas is the time of year when the whole world is aware of Jesus Christ. This fun-to-make banner will provide a way for the children to proclaim Jesus' birth and publicly honor Him. Encourage the children to hang their banners on their front door.

Before you begin the activity explain to your children that a banner is a piece of cloth bearing an emblem, a motto, or a slogan. It is used to proclaim, announce, or declare publicly. Read the Christmas story in Luke 2 and point out the excitement of the angels "good tidings of great joy which will be to ALL people"—the birth of the Savior, Jesus Christ the Lord.

As the children plan their banner remind them of the joy and excitement of Jesus' birth—God coming to earth in the form of a baby! Help them choose ways of proclaiming that joy and excitement. Use simple words and phrases.

purpose

And the angel said unto them, Fear not: for, behold, I bring you good tidings of great joy, which shall be to all people.
Luke 2:10

Glory to God in the highest, and on earth peace, good will toward men.
Luke 2:14

Scripture

christmas

materials

- 18" x 20" prewashed white or pastel cotton cloth
- 5-6 rubber bands
- 36" x 3/8" wooden dowel
- 3 yard ribbon
- paper towels
- newspapers
- 3-5 colors of tempera paint
- small sponge squares
- permanent markers
- clothesline
- clothespins

preparation

1. Sew a 1" hem along the vertical sides and bottom.
2. Sew a hem along the top that is open on both sides to allow the wooden dowel to slip through later.
3. Measure and cut the wooden dowels into 18" lengths.
4. Measure and cut the ribbon into four 18" lengths leaving one 36" length.
5. Mix the paint to a watery consistency.
6. Assemble and prepare the painting table.
7. Anchor a clothesline for drying the hanging.

procedure

1. Crumple a paper towel into a ball.
2. Slip the ball under a portion of cloth to make a small lump. Twist the cloth around the paper ball and secure it with a rubber band.
3. Repeat this procedure several times. Keep the lumps 6" apart.
4. Using a sponge dipped into one color of tempera paint, dab it onto each lump and below the rubber band. Don't drown the cloth but allow the paint to flow.
5. Change to a second color for another lump. Continue to use the tempera paint for all the lumps.
6. Release all the rubber bands. Hang the cloth on the clothesline to dry.
7. Study the pattern and design. Determine if new lumps need to be added or overlapped.
8. Dry iron the cloth lightly from the back.
9. Use a permanent marker to neatly print in large letters a short message or word. Example: Rejoice!, Jesus is born!
10. Slip the dowel through the top hem.
11. On each side of the banner tie (2) 18" length ribbons at different lengths.
12. Secure the banner with the 36" ribbon tied to both ends. Hang.

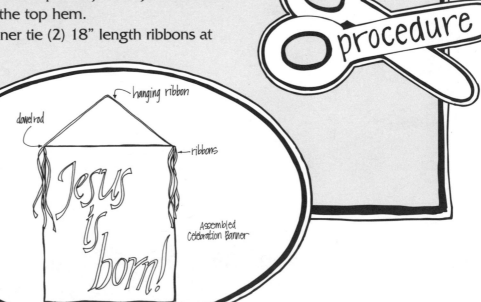

Assembled Celebration Banner

CHRISTMAS DOOR DECORATION

Decorating for Christmas is fun for all ages. This simple Christmas craft is a perfect vehicle for a discussion that could lead a child to accept Jesus Christ as Savior. Begin the discussion by asking the children, "What is a door? What is the purpose of a door?"

Explain to the children that a door is a moveable structure. A door shuts off or opens up one area to another.

Revelation 3:20 tells us that Jesus "stands at the door" of our heart and "knocks". Jesus does not push His way into our heart and life. He waits to be invited in. If you choose to open the door of your heart and invite Him into your life you will enjoy His presence forever.

Finish the discussion by explaining that God's Spirit may be gently knocking at the door of someone's heart today. Reassure them not to be afraid to open the door of their heart to Jesus now. Tell them that if there is someone who would like to do that you would like to meet with them when everyone else has begun the craft.

purpose

scripture

A door was opened unto me of the Lord,
2 Corinthians 2:12

And pray for us, too,
that God may open a door for our message.
Colossians 4:3, NIV

I know thy works: behold, I have set before thee an open door,
and no man can shut it: for thou hast a little strength,
and hast kept my word, and hast not denied my name.
Revelation 3:8

christmas

materials

- (2) 8 1/2" x 11" colored felt pieces
- sharp scissors
- patterns - hanger, star, bell
- glue
- sequins
- trims
- glitter
- fine tip marker

procedure

1. Draw around the patterns with the marker onto 2 different colors of felt. Cut out the pieces.
2. Place the smaller piece on top of the larger piece and cut a cross through the center of both thicknesses.
3. Glue the smaller felt piece to the larger felt piece.
4. Decorate and trim.

41

CHRISTMAS DOOR DECORATION (STAR PATTERN)

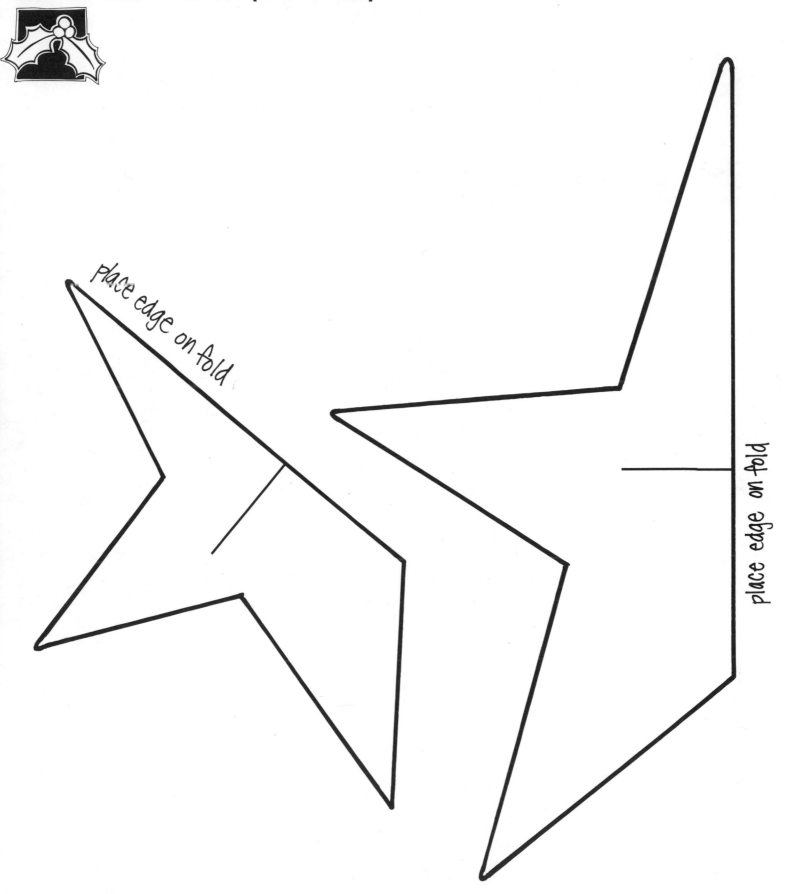

place edge on fold

place edge on fold

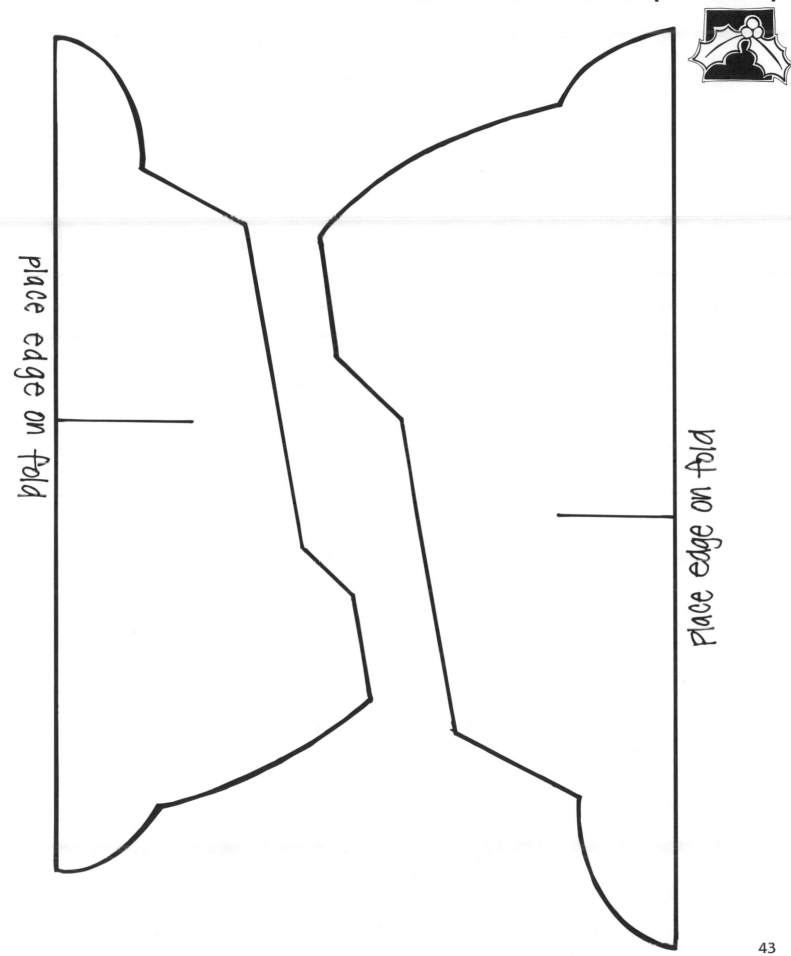

place edge on fold

Place edge on fold

Jesus is the Light

CHRISTMAS CANDLE DECORATION

Why do we see so many candles at Christmas? Candles produce a wonderful glow. They light the way for someone stumbling in the darkness.

Talk with the children about Jesus being called the "Light of the World." Remind them that just as the wise men were drawn to Jesus by the bright star in the night sky, people today who are living in the darkness of sin and deception are drawn by the Holy Spirit to Jesus. As His light shines into their hearts sin is revealed, truth destroys error, and His love brings mercy and grace. Then, like the wise men, they can worship Him as the King of Kings Lord of Lords—Savior of the world.

purpose

Scripture

*Then spake Jesus again unto them,
saying, I am the light of the world:
he that followeth me shall not walk in darkness,
but shall have the light of life.
John 8:12*

*In him was life; and the life was the light of men.
John 1:4*

*Let your light so shine before men,
that they may see your good works,
and glorify your Father which is in heaven.
Matthew 5:16*

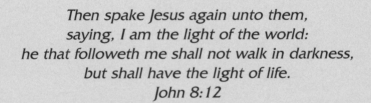

christmas

materials

- 9" X 12" construction paper
- construction paper scraps
- markers
- glue
- scissors
- pencil
- glitter stickers
- trims
- gold foil paper
- 5" posterboard squares

procedure

1. Decide what kind of candle you want to make by experimenting with the 9" x 12" construction paper. Roll it horizontally overlapping edges for a short candle. Roll it vertically overlapping edges for a tall candle. Cut the paper to adjust for width and less overlapping.
2. Lay the paper flat on the table. Use construction paper scraps, markers, and different items for trim to decorate.
3. Roll the decorated construction paper sheet into a tube and glue the edges together.
4. Make small slits all around the bottom edge and fold the flaps outward.
5. Set the tube on the 5" square with the flaps down on the cardboard. Glue the flaps to the cardboard.
6. Make 2 slits on each side of the top edge of the tube.
7. Make a flame from the gold foil paper and fasten it into the slits.
8. Make several tube candles of various heights. Display them in a grouping with evergreens surrounding their bases.

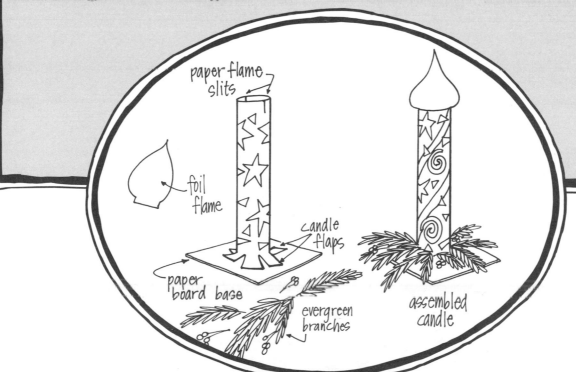

Helping others

TREE OF HANDS

This fun Christmas craft will get the children thinking about how they use their hands. God gives each of us two hands to do many helpful things. Ask the children to list things they do with their hands that help others during the Christmas season. Then expand your list to include helpful activities they do with their hands all year long. Be sure to include activities at home, at school, at church, and in the neighborhood. Be specific. Emphasize to your children that whatever they do with their hands God wants them to do their very best. Their attitude should be that of doing the task unto the Lord not necessarily just for mom, their teacher, their neighbor, or their friend.

For younger children use the melody of London Bridge for this song:

Jesus gives me helping hands

Helping hands

Helping hands

Jesus gives me helping hands

I can _____. (pray, dust, read, wash)

(Use an action to illustrate the word.)

Whatsoever thy hand findeth to do,
do it with thy might.
Ecclesiastes 9:10

She opens her arms to the poor
and extends her hands to the needy.
Proverbs 31:20, NIV

Scripture

christmas

materials

- 1 bottle textile medium
- red, green, and yellow acrylic paint
- 3 margarine container lids
- prewashed white sweatshirt for each child
- Q-tips™
- sponges
- star pattern
- 18" red satin ribbon
- 10" x 18" posterboard for each child
- safety pin
- hanger
- newspaper
- glitter paint (optional)
- brushes
- paper towels

preparation

1. Prepare the painting area with newspaper, paper towels, Q-tips™, sponges, brushes, lids, and paints.
2. Mix 1 part textile medium to 2 parts acrylic paint. Place each color on a separate lid.
3. Prepare the clean up area if you do not have a sink.
4. Prepare an area to hang or lay the finished sweatshirt.
5. Use the star pattern and make several stars out of sponges. Place them near the yellow paint.
6. Cut sponge squares or use brushes to spread paint. Place these near the green paint.
7. Place the Q-tips™ near the red paint.
8. Insert the posterboard into the sweatshirt to prevent the paint from bleeding through.

If you are working with a group of children have them gather around you to watch as you demonstrate the activity before they begin.

procedure

1. At the paint table the child will paint one hand green using the sponge or brush dipped in green paint. Do not paint too thickly.
2. Begin at the bottom of the sweatshirt front. Direct their hand and lay it flat on the sweatshirt and press. (Note placement on illustration.)
3. Repeat the procedure until a tree is formed from handprints. Wash hands.
4. Using a Q-tip™ dipped in red paint dot the green tree. Let dry thoroughly.
5. To top the tree choose between a bow made from the red ribbon or printing a yellow star with the star sponge.
6. Be sure the paint is completely dry before removing the cardboard. Allow several hours.

TREE OF HANDS PATTERN

3. paint yellow star or tie red ribbon

1. paint hands (bottom to top)

2. paint red dots

God Sends Angels

PAPER ANGEL DECORATION

The word "angel" in Hebrew and Greek means "messenger". Children are always curious about angels. What do they look like? Can we see them? What do they do?

purpose

Use this simple craft near Christmas to talk with your children about angels. To insure they learn the truth concerning them use your Bible to look up Scriptures and Bible stories with references to angels. Read them together. Help the children write down the basic truths they learn.

These might include:

1. Angels are not the spirits of dead people. Angels are spirit beings created by God to deliver His message or do work commanded by Him. (Nehemiah 9:6, Psalm 103:20)

2. We are not to worship angels. Though they are powerful God is in authority over them. We are to call on God for help not the angels. (1 Peter 3:22, Colossians 2:18)

Scripture

For by him were all things created, that are in heaven, and that are in earth, visible and invisible, whether they be thrones, or dominions, or principalities, or powers: all things were created by him, and for him.
Colossians 1:16

For he shall give his angels charge over thee, to keep thee in all thy ways.
They shall bear thee up in their hands, lest thou dash thy foot against a stone.
Psalm 91:11-12

Be not forgetful to entertain strangers:
for thereby some have entertained angels unawares.
Hebrews 13:2

christmas

materials

- angel pattern
- 8" x 12" white construction paper
- glue, gold & silver glitter
- fine tip markers
- pencil
- scissors
- paper plate
- yellow & brown yarn
- paper punch

preparation

1. Prepare the pattern.
2. Prepare an area to work with glitter. Lay out the glue, paper plates, and glitter.

procedure

1. Draw around the pattern on the white construction paper. Cut out the angel. Mark the "x" on each side.
2. Use markers to draw the face and hands. Use yarn for hair. Print name and year on the angel's skirt.
3. At the glitter area apply the glue to the areas where you want glitter.
4. Lay the angel on a paper plate. Sprinkle the glitter to completely cover the glue.
5. Lift and shake excess glitter off angel and into the paper plate.
6. Place the "x's" together and glue.
7. Punch a hole in the top of the angel and hang with yarn.

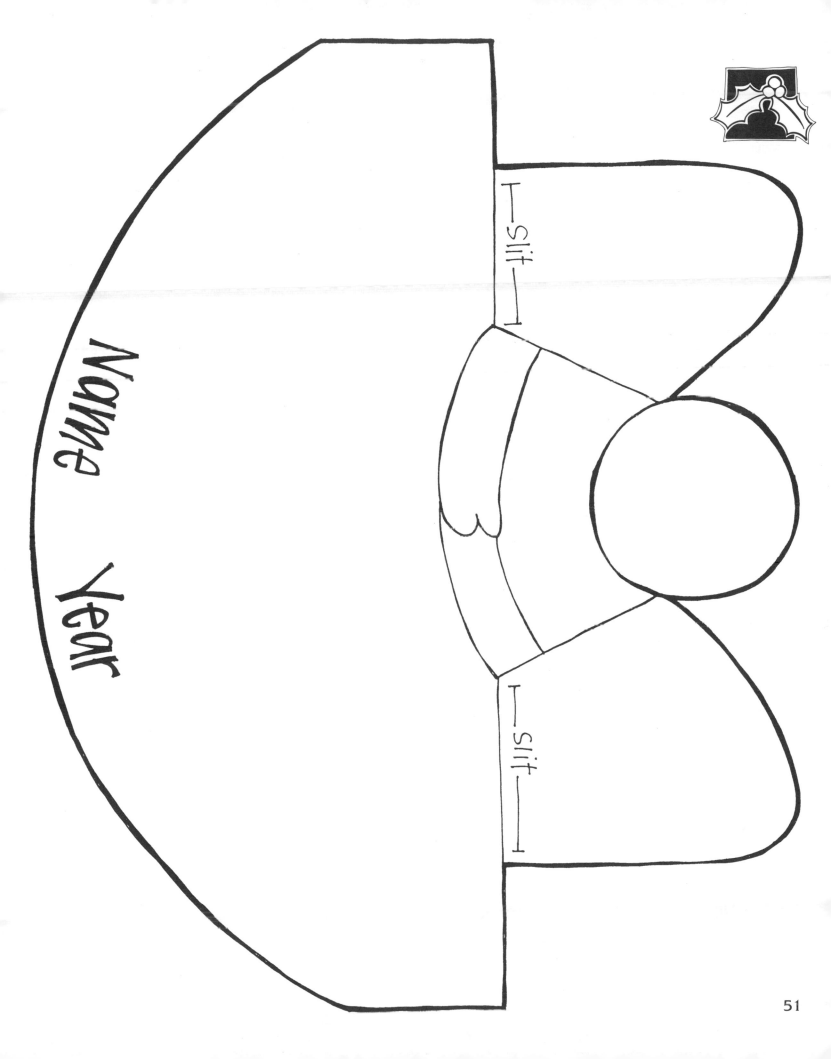

Name

Year

slit

slit

CHECK WITH YOUR LOCAL CHRISTIAN BOOKSTORE FOR THESE OTHER EXCITING EDUCATIONAL RESOURCES!

Other arts and crafts resources for ages 6 and up:

Celebrate Learning About God and His Word	0805402462
Celebrate God's Word About Me	0805402470
Celebrate Walking with Jesus	0805402489

Academic activity books:

Red Letter Days, Special Activities and Devotions for Every Letter of the Alphabet (Preschool)	0805402349
God Made You Sense-ational, Special Activities for Teaching the 5 Senses (Ages 5-10)	0805402357

Science experiments that point elementary-age children to the Creator!

The Glad Scientist Discovers the Creator	0805402640
The Glad Scientist Visits Outer Space	0805402659

Complete Bible lessons for teachers on the go!

Teacher Take Out, Grades 1-6	0805400427
Teacher Take Out, Preschool	0805400435
Teacher Take Out 2, Grades 1-6	0805402284
Teacher Take Out 2, Preschool	0805402004
Teacher Take Out 3, Grades 1-6	0805402446
Teacher Take Out 3, Preschool	0805402438

Activity pages for those "in-between" times:

When the Well Runs Dry, Ideas and Activities for 4's and 5's	0805478906
When the Well Runs Dry, Ideas and Activities for 1st & 2nd Grades	0805478914
When the Well Runs Dry, Ideas and Activities for 3rd & 4th Grades	0805478922
When the Well Runs Dry, Ideas and Activities for 5th & 6th Grades	0805478930
When the Well Runs Dry Again, Ideas and Activities for Grades 1-6	0805479333
When the Well Runs Dry Again, Ideas for Preschool Teaching Centers	0805479341
When the Well Runs Totally & Completely Dry, Ideas and Activities for Grades 1-6	0805400192
When the Well Runs Totally & Completely Dry, Preschool Recipes, Fingerplays, and Activities	0805400206

Coloring Books for children of all ages:

Ancient Heroes - Noah	0805400443
Ancient Heroes - Moses	0805400451
Ancient Heroes - Esther	080540046X
Ancient Heroes - David and the Leaders of Israel	0805400478

Teaching Posters books:

Big Book of Teaching Posters: Community Helpers	0805402667
Big Book of Teaching Posters: Nature	0805402675
Inspirational Poster Book for Children	0805402683